Confirmation of a Divine Call

Confirmation of a Divine Call

Miriam Passmore

XULON PRESS

Xulon Press
2301 Lucien Way #415
Maitland, FL 32751
407.339.4217
www.xulonpress.com

For more information contact:
MIRIAM PASSMORE
Email: outofthefireministries@yahoo.com
Facebook: Miriam Passmore
Instagram/miriampassmore

Paperback ISBN-13: 978-1-66287-693-6
Ebook ISBN-13: 978-1-66287-694-3

Dedications

To my mother, Ms. Annette Passmore, and my father, the (late) Willie Passmore, Sr.

To my children: Shena and Darius

To my siblings: Cassandra, (the late) Willie Jr., Anthony,

Frederick, Nancy, Geraldine, and Demetrice

Special thanks:

To: My spiritual father, Apostle Kevin McAnulty, thank you so much for always taking time out of your busy schedule to pray for and counsel me. He recognized the call of God on my life and has always been supportive of me and only a phone call away. I appreciate your kindness!

Special thanks to:

Mr. Tom and Jean Dunn

Confirmation of a Divine Call

Pastor Bonita Fagin

Ms. Florence Ahrens

The (late) David Cox

Table of Contents

Foreword

What a miracle God did several years ago as He took back what the enemy thought he had stolen. God saved, delivered, and healed a young African American woman named Miriam Passmore. I saw this happen over a short time as she determined to risk rejection from people in the Christian world as well as the world of homosexuality. What she found was love, acceptance, and forgiveness from God, the church, and people who cared about her and her family. She would no longer have to live a double life as God replaced her pain with joy.

I have known Miriam and been her pastor for several years now, beginning our relationship at the altar at Christian Family Worship Center of South Florida. She has grown spiritually like a rocket blasting off and is a relentless pursuer of truth and love in Jesus. She loves the anointing and allows God, her heavenly Father, to utilize her testimony to reach and win countless people to make decisions for the kingdom of heaven. She has evangelized in schools, the streets, government meetings, prayer services, prisons, Christian radio and television stations, and churches with the gospel of Jesus

Christ. She died to the old Miriam and has embraced the Christ in her to become a new creature who is a feminine example of inner and outer beauty. Her countenance radiates with a precious humility of dependence on the Lord like no one I know, and she is a pure-hearted daughter of Zion whose goal now is to please God. Miriam is a willing vessel who shares a hope that will not disappoint as her faith is set toward Christ and her walk is steady with the Holy Spirit as her guide. She has shown that she is vulnerable as a human but staunch in her stand as a witness to Jesus for others to see and follow as an example.

Miriam's life story will move you to tears and fill you with joy as you see her triumphant victory as the result of God calling and choosing her to be His poster child of deliverance from lesbianism. Her testimony proves that God loves the person in any type of bondage and is not a respecter of persons. He can and will deliver those who are sincere and honest with Him and willing to be discipled and accountable to their authority figures. I may not be a lot older than Miriam Passmore, but I am proud to call her a spiritual daughter and am so glad she chose to come and fellowship and risk the step of faith it took for her to be free. She is a dear saint, and I can't wait to see the rewards of her ministry one day in heaven as I believe many will say that her testimony gave them the courage to come out of the darkness into the glorious light of the kingdom of God.

I highly recommend this testimonial to those who have loved ones who you may have thought were impossible to reach. Romans 8:30 communicates the written heart of God as it reads, "Moreover who He did predestinate, them He also called: and whom He called, them He also justified: and whom He justified, them He also glorified." He has desired all men to be saved, and if Jesus does not return too soon, Miriam is going to bring a few along with her from all over the world as they bring glory to God.

Kevin D. McAnulty
Senior Pastor
Heartland Church

What Was I?

I lived a lesbian lifestyle as a male impersonator for twenty years. I can remember as early as first grade, I had fantasies of being sexually involved with my schoolteacher. I was young and didn't fully understand what sex was, but I knew I had a problem. I became attracted to girls in my class but couldn't tell my secret to anyone because I knew I should be attracted to boys (I was confused and afraid). I came from a large family; my parents had eight children, four girls and four boys. I loved my sisters and brothers, but I was more involved with my brothers' activities. I never had the desire to do girl things—they were just too boring. I continued to hang around with boys, and I started to pick up their habits. In the process, I was losing my identity as a girl.

One day while I was playing with some other kids, it felt like an invisible force tried to overpower me. After that, I began to cry, and I just shut down. At the time, I didn't know it was a spirit that would control my life for years to come. While I was still very young and desperate for help, I picked up a magazine in the kitchen. As I began to look through the back of it, I saw a phone number of someone who said, "If you have any problems, contact this number." I called the number, and a woman answered the phone. I began to cry and told her the things that were happening to me and that I didn't want to be this way. She told me that someone had put a curse on me. I immediately hung up the phone and cried even harder. I was too ashamed to talk to anybody.

One Christmas, my mother bought me a baby doll. I shoved her in the corner and began to play with my brothers and their toys. Eventually, I started having girls as friends, but I still didn't want anyone to find out about my true feelings. I was able to hide them from everyone for a long time. Years after that, a man I respected and trusted took advantage of me and sexually abused me. This went on for a long time, and it made me bitter toward men. It appeared to me that men were always taking advantage of women and that women seemed to be weak. Not realizing what was going on in my life, I began to take on the identity of the person who had molested me.

As I got older, my desire to be with women became stronger. I started playing football with my brothers and began wearing boys' clothing. I felt embarrassed to put on a dress because I believed God had made me different. Afraid that my mother would find out what was going on, I began to suppress my feelings, but deep down inside, I was hurting. I often thought to myself, *Is there anybody else like me, or am I all alone?* Although I was able to maintain normal friendships with girls, I felt alone because I wasn't able to be honest about my true feelings. I was afraid of being rejected. At times, the pressure was overwhelming, so much so that at the age of thirteen, I turned to alcohol to drown my pain. I started drinking a six-pack of beer a day and soon was on my way to becoming an alcoholic.

In my early high school years, I began to skip classes. I tried smoking marijuana along with drinking alcohol because it put me in another world where I didn't have to deal with me. At the age of sixteen, I became sexually involved with an older woman. Both of us knew we had a strong attraction to one another, and I felt relieved because, for once, someone else understood me. I wasn't alone, and I could share my heart. I expressed my feelings to her, and she did the same. But soon, people began to tease me about her. My secret was out. It hurt so bad that I started resenting her. I then became involved with another girl from school. The scorn and the ridicule caused me to drink even more. I often thought, *Is there a God? If there is, why is He causing me so much pain?*

The most important thing to me at the time was that I didn't want my mother to find out, but she did. My friend from school had gone off to college and had written letters to me. When my mother became suspicious, she read one of the letters. I never wanted to break her heart, but this traumatized her terribly. I started to withdraw from my family, after I graduated from high school, I went my own way and tried dating men to take away my desire to be with women. While I was seeking my womanhood, I got involved with an older man. He had knowledge of my lifestyle and promised that he could change me. It's important to understand that having sex with a man cannot heal any woman from lesbianism. It takes the blood of JESUS! And in my case, it only made the situation worse. I continued struggling to be "normal" and stayed up crying many nights. I got pregnant and had a baby girl. As my daughter grew up, we didn't have a mother-daughter relationship because I was afraid to get close to her. Being a mother reminded me of the little girl inside of me, and I had mixed emotions about life and people. I couldn't understand why I was born a girl and had desires to be with girls. My mind told me one thing, but my body wanted to do something else.

The man I was dating was a drug dealer, and eventually, I started using cocaine. At the time, I made many friends because of my involvement with him. I wanted acceptance no matter the cost, but deep within my heart, I knew people were hanging around just to get what they could from me. Essentially, I was buying their love. When the drugs and money ran out, so did my so-called "friends." I moved deeper into lesbianism, and some of the women in my life were very abusive and controlling. I thought this was the way I was doomed to live and that I needed to make the best of it, even if it meant I suffered greatly. I encountered lots of other homosexuals and concluded that I had been born gay and that this was the way God had made me. I didn't try to fix it anymore. All I would do is get frustrated and get drunk. Deep inside, I couldn't handle fighting a battle I had little hope of winning.

I often looked in the mirror and stared at myself. I looked like a girl, but believed I was a man. I could never figure it out. I started coming out of the closet more. I dressed like a man and started acting like one. I became so bold in my lesbianism that my butch name was, "Granddaddy." I earned a reputation of being the grandest stud in town. I continued to drink and ended up getting pregnant again, this time with a baby boy, and I felt so ashamed. Most women would be happy to find out they were pregnant, but I was thinking of myself and how it would affect my standing and tarnish my reputation as a lesbian! I hid my pregnancy from everyone for as long as I could. When I began to show in my sixth month, I avoided everybody. I knew I would be interrogated by people, and I had no answers to give them. A part of me was sad, yet another part was happy. Was it a sign from God, reminding me that He had created me to be a woman? I didn't know.

My life was getting too complicated, and I convinced myself that I had to change. I wanted to be a whole woman. One night, I went out to a bar with a friend and his girlfriend and told them I was tired of living the homosexual life. I felt so relieved. They were happy for me (although they'd never made me feel badly before). I stayed strong for a while, avoiding other women. I wanted to be a good mother to my children but ended up falling deeper than I had before. The drugs, the alcohol, the women, everything seemed to come at me even stronger. At this point, I had lost all hope of being a woman. Although I didn't have a relationship with God at the time, I believed that He existed. Again, I questioned Him—why was I this way, and what had I ever done to Him to cause me to live such a painful life?

Who Was I?

I believed that God had made a mistake when He made me. There was a battle going on inside of me that I didn't know how to fight. Just as faith as small as a mustard seed can do much, so can a small amount of evil if we let it. The thing that had been fighting for control of my mind since childhood came to its fullness, and I didn't have the strength to fight it anymore. I gave up, no longer having the will to try.

Knowing I would be ridiculed and scorned, I was constantly on guard, ready to defend myself. I needed to be hard and tough, but on the inside, I was crying out for help. I struggled with fear and low self-esteem and became more and more emotionally dependent upon women. I assured myself that I must have been born this way; otherwise, why would I have these strong feelings toward women?

As I lost my identity as a woman, I developed a strong masculine personality. I couldn't handle being a mother mentally, so I exchanged my love for my children with giving them material things, believing I was doing the right thing. (I didn't see the pain and suffering this caused my children.) But buying things for them on their birthdays and holidays only temporarily helped take away the guilt I felt.

I decided what would be normal was to become a "father" to my children. I felt as if I were their father, so figured it had to be right. Whenever I saw a man with his wife and children, it made me angry. Why? Because in my heart, I knew I had given birth to two children and men don't have babies. The battle in my mind raged on, and fear and pain caused me to become cold, even toward my children.

Job 6:11

What strength do I have left, that I should wait (and hope)? And what is ahead of me, that I should be patient and endure?

Psalm 109:22

For I am suffering and needy, and my heart is wounded, within me.

Desperation

I grew tired of living in a make-believe world. I felt comfortable around other gay people and felt strength in their presence, but once I was alone, the hurt and pain would begin to surface again. I was emotionally disturbed and didn't know or like the person I had become. I didn't want to be a homosexual, but I felt trapped. Alcohol and cocaine seemed to be the only means of escape from anguish, so I tried to stay drunk and high.

One night, I couldn't handle the pain any longer and got very drunk. Suicidal thoughts ran through my mind. I was driving down the turnpike, and I heard a voice saying, "Run into that light pole and kill yourself! It's the only way out!" I began to cry, but I couldn't bring myself to do it. I managed to resist the urge to kill myself, but after that, I isolated myself from everyone I knew and began to search for more people who were just like me—people I could relate to because they were homosexuals. I wanted to overcome the shame of being a lesbian. Despite this, there were times when I needed someone else with me so I could go certain places and still feel safe. I worried about what other people thought of me and was afraid of being ridiculed or scorned because I was a woman who portrayed herself as a man.

Society didn't make my identity problem any easier. People always made smart remarks pertaining to homosexuality. People who attended church would constantly condemn and ridicule homosexuals. This caused me to hate many people. They didn't know or care about my pain, and yet they judged me and others like me. They never took the time to find out what made me do the things I did. Some people even went so far as to say that gay people should be killed. In some places, gays were being killed or beaten because of their behavior. I continued to struggle to make the best of my painful lifestyle.

Early one morning, I was leaving Ft. Lauderdale after spending the weekend partying at several gay clubs. I was traveling south on I-95 when I somehow made the wrong turn. I exited into downtown Miami and ended up underneath the bypass. To my surprise, people were sleeping out on the sidewalks and in parking spaces. I rode around in the area for a few minutes, just staring. I had never seen anything like this before. I left and went on my way but couldn't seem to let it go. A few weeks later, I decided to take a trip back to Miami. As I drove up to the fenced-in area where I'd been before, I saw two men and a woman lying on the street. I got out of my car, and one of the men saw me and started to walk away. I yelled for him to stop. The first thing he asked me was if I was affiliated with a church. I told him that I wasn't, and he decided to stop and talk to me. He told me his name was Joe. There was a hole in the fence, so I walked through it, sat down on a milk crate, and started talking to him. He introduced me to his friends. During our conversation, Joe told me that this was the first time he had been treated like a human being in a long time. He told me that people would come up to the fence and throw food over it like they were animals. No one would take the time to try to help them.

My visits were frequent, and I developed a friendship with Joe, Rose, and Austin. I found myself always talking to them about God and often took them food and clothing I had collected from my co-workers. People from my job became interested and traveled with me to Miami on Thanksgiving and other holidays to make sure that Joe and the others had a decent meal. I did this for a couple of years until they closed off the roads. I even sent letters to the governor asking for assistance for the people.

One day, I decided to go by myself. I didn't have any food, but I wanted to spend time with my friends. When I got there, a recliner was in the middle of the sidewalk, so I sat in it, and we talked about God and our lives. All of a sudden, I felt very comfortable, as if I belonged there. Fear gripped my heart, so I jumped up and left. I kept thinking, *Am I going to end up homeless? Why do I feel so comfortable with these people?* I didn't say a word about it to anyone and stayed away from Miami for a while. One day, I began to meditate and try to figure out what was happening. A soft voice whispered to me, "These are the people you can relate to—the brokenhearted, the rejected, the outcasts." I began to think of my own hurts and wept. God was preparing me for His purpose. The next time I drove to Miami, I couldn't find Joe. Maybe he got saved. Maybe our talks about God started him on his own journey to faith.

In 1989, I decided I wanted to start being part of the Annual Gay Ball. Every Easter Sunday for many years, gay men would come out, and drag queens would perform in an extravaganza for the homosexual community. No one had ever represented the lesbians, so that year, I dressed in my tuxedo, top hat, and cane, going all the way "out." I won trophies every year for best dressed stud, the number one stud, and the grandest stud of the year. We rode around throughout the city in stretch limousines. The community couldn't wait to come out and support us. I started recruiting other women to be part of the ball. Most of the people who participated were very talented. We had singers, dancers, and models. One year, I reflected on the fact that my children were getting older and that my daughter, who was around thirteen, was becoming a young lady. The morning of the ball, my heart wasn't in it. Usually, I would hold a party the night before and spend the day drinking, looking forward to getting dressed up in my tuxedo. This time, however, I seemed to be just going through the motions.

The afternoon came, and the limo picked up me and my friends. When we arrived at the ball, hundreds of people were there waiting to cheer us on. As we got out of the limo, I saw my daughter. Although there was a crowd of people, our eyes met, and I suddenly felt guilty. The guilt was greater than the desire I had to be with women. I didn't know it at the time, but the Holy Spirit was bringing deep conviction to my heart. I remember thinking, *How can she call me her mother when I'm dressed in a tuxedo?* That was the last time I attended the gay ball. I knew I had to change.

At work, I befriended an older gentleman who took me under his wing as if I was his own daughter. Our friendship continued to grow stronger over time, and although I was sure he knew about my lifestyle, he never condemned me. He was always trying to help me with anything I needed. Every Christmas, he made sure my kids had lots of toys. Sadly, he was a heavy smoker, and it eventually made him very sick. I took him to the hospital, and he needed an operation on his lungs. Somehow, I knew that would be the last time I would see him alive. When he died, I felt as if a part of me had died too. My grief was so deep that I eventually turned to the Bible just to get some comfort, and God used this man's death to cause me to examine my life.

As I began to search throughout Scripture, I stumbled onto Leviticus 18:22, which says, "Thou shalt not lie with mankind, as with womankind: it is an abomination." I immediately flipped the pages. I was okay with reading anything in the Bible except when it came to homosexuality. Did this mean the Lord hated me? No, it didn't. But, at this point, I didn't understand God's balance of mercy and truth. The saying is true, "Mercy without truth deceives, and truth without mercy destroys." Oh, how I wish people would seek the face of God and find His all-encompassing love, truth, and power to heal and set them free! God loves the sinner, but He hates the sin, so He provides a means of escape and cleansing for every person. I found myself reading the Bible more and more because it gave me great peace despite missing my friend. One day at work, I had an argument with a coworker. I had read a verse the night before in which Jesus told His disciples to "deny yourself, take up your cross and follow after me." Without realizing it, I was beginning to see answers to my problems in the Bible and was beginning to obey the Word of God. When I ran into my co-worker later, I greeted her with a smile. It was as if a thousand pounds had been lifted off my shoulders.

Little by little, I continued obeying God's Word, and He began changing my heart. The more my heart changed, the more I was able to understand the Word. I realized that He didn't hate me but that my behavior grieved Him, and I began to understand that He loved me so much He gave up His only Son so that I could be made whole. **John 3:16-17** says, *"For God so (greatly) loved and dearly prized the world that He (even) gave His (One and) only begotten Son, that whoever* *believes and trusts in Him (as Savior) shall not perish but have eternal life. For God did not send His Son into the world to judge and condemn the world (that is, to initiate the final judgment of the world) but that the world might be saved through Him."* [Italics added] I began taking His Word personally.

Once I began my relationship with Him, I realized that I had been rebelling against the Living God, and it made me weep uncontrollably. I repented and asked the Lord to please forgive me of my sins and humbled myself as I embraced His Word. While I was doing this, He was preparing my heart. I became so discontented with my lifestyle that I didn't know what was happening to me. I tried blaming it on a tough work schedule and not getting enough rest. One day, I went to a park for a day of relaxation but found I was more uncomfortable than ever. I got to the point that I didn't like to drink anymore because alcohol seemed to turn my stomach, and I eventually stopped drinking completely. As I started praying and reading the Bible more, I found that I didn't want to curse. I was falling in love with Jesus through His Word and realizing that He is the Word. *"In the beginning (before all time) was the Word (Christ), and the Word was with God, and the Word was God Himself"* (**John 1:1**).

One day, a young man at work came up to me and asked if he could pray for me, and I said yes. His name was David, and he seemed to be almost everywhere I went. I'd look up, and there he'd be, smiling. I didn't know it, but David was part of a prayer group at work. A few men would gather every day at noon to pray during their lunch break. A long-time friend and co-worker had asked David to pray for me, so he'd been watching me and deliberately putting himself in my path so he could talk to me about the love of God. The day he approached me and asked if he could pray for me, he was able to tell me things that no one else knew. He told me things that had happened to me as a child, and I began to weep. After he finished praying, he led me to the Lord and said, "God is going to use you to bring many people into His kingdom." I didn't understand what he meant at the time.

As I watched him walk away, I thought of him as an angel sent by God. And then, for some reason, anger started to rise up in me against him, but I resisted it. All of a sudden, a great peace came over me. I began to lose my desire to sleep with women. My stomach would feel like I was having labor pains whenever I tried to indulge in sex with a woman, and it hurt so bad that I would crawl on the floor and cry out to God. I couldn't do it anymore. It was the Holy Spirit working in me.

I was at work early one morning, and my supervisor was giving us our assignments. As part of my job, I walked to the third level of a building directly in front the water tower. It was a beautiful morning, and I could see the ocean from there. I stood there for a moment, meditating and trying to comprehend all the things that had been happening to me. I looked up at the tower, and the word "WATER" stood out as if it had jumped into my mind. Then it seemed as though a voice started telling me to get baptized. Wanting to ignore the voice, I ran down the stairs and tried to find anyone I could to talk to, hoping this would make it go away, but it didn't stop. I tried talking out loud, but this didn't help either. Finally, I just said, "Okay, Lord! Here I am." Although I had experienced a divine encounter, I was afraid. I knew in my heart that once I made a commitment, I couldn't go back.

Philippians 3:13

Brothers and sisters, I do not consider that I have made it my own yet; but one thing I do: forgetting what lies behind and reaching forward to what lies ahead.

Adoption

I stepped out in faith, not knowing, not seeing, but somehow trusting God and His Word. I asked different people at work about church and eventually began visiting one in the Perrine Area, where I would be baptized. I joined the church and attended faithfully, but things came to a standstill in my life, and I began to lose the desire to go to church. It bothered me because in my heart, I knew I needed more freedom but didn't know how to get it. I needed more than religious forms; I needed inner healing.

I talked to David about it, and he encouraged me to try another church. When I found one, I didn't know what to expect, but my heart was hungry for more of God. As I walked up the sidewalk, a young man greeted me. He had a warm smile on his face, and he seemed very kind. As soon as I entered the doors of the auditorium, a warm, loving feeling enveloped me. The service started, and the music was beautiful. I saw black people, white people, Hispanic people, and people of all types worshiping God together. The love of God was radiating out of people. When it came time for the pastor to speak, he walked up and down the aisles, talking about "the anointing." I had never heard that word before but soon would experience it.

Several leaders lined up across the front with the pastor, and they gave people the opportunity to come up for prayer. He began to pray for me, and I couldn't stop crying. Other people who had come up were also crying and embracing each other. The Spirit of God was moving upon our hearts...I knew the Lord had heard my cry and that He was answering my prayers. As I stood there experiencing the awesome, powerful presence of God, I realized that this was what I'd been missing.

I continued to fellowship at the church, and one Sunday morning, I took my daughter with me. As the pastor spoke, the prophetic anointing was upon him. He said, "There is a woman in here this morning, and God has sent you here." Even though there must have been at least 400 people in the room, as he spoke more about this "woman," I knew he was talking about me. He said, "Come up here; the Spirit of the Lord is here to help you." I stood up and made my way to the front, not knowing what to expect. After I got there, he put his hands on me and began to pray. I can remember him saying, "God is going to change your lifestyle." I fell to the floor on my back. The pastor called for some of the women in the room to come up and help him. He then placed a Bible on my stomach and began to pray and quote scriptures. Tears filled my eyes, and the women who were praying for me looked like angels. They were all gathered around me as if they were guarding me.

As the pastor continued to pray, my back came up from the floor. I started screaming and crying, saying," God, please help me!" One woman placed her hand on me, and my stomach began to bounce like a ball. As they kept praying, a war was going on in the spiritual realm, and God was delivering me. During this time, the limbs of my body seemed to be disconnected from me, as if someone inside was controlling them. At one point, I thought someone had taken me by the arm because I was sliding across the floor. No one had, but something was attempting to pull me away. The people kept praying, and soon, it was over. I lay flat on the floor; both the pastor and I were soaking wet. I felt empty, as if I'd just given birth to a baby, and I didn't have the strength to stand by myself. Some of the people picked me up and carried me to my seat. My daughter was crying because she didn't understand what was going on. One of the ministers sat with her and explained to her what was happening to me. When I went home, I went to bed for two days and did little else but fill myself with the Word of God.

The next Wednesday, I went to Bible study at the church. The pastor said he was glad I came because he wanted to explain what had taken place on Sunday. He told me that I had been delivered from thirteen evil spirits and wanted me to know that God Himself had accomplished the work.

Shortly afterwards, I was invited by a co-worker and his wife, the Dunn's, to come to their home and share about the good things that God had done in my life. My family and friends came. This was the very first time I had spoken in front of people, and from that day on, God began to open doors for me to share my testimony. Mr. Tom Dunn and his wife Jean later became my spiritual God-parents and have had a major impact on my life.

Psalms 147:3

He heals the brokenhearted and binds up their wounds (healing their pain and comforting their sorrow).

Psalms 30:2

O Lord, My God, I cried to You for help and You have healed me.

Psalms 107:20

He sent His word and healed them and rescued them from their destruction.

The Process of Healing

S oon after, I joined the church and received counseling from the pastor and some of the elders. During one visit, I told the pastor about some of the things that I had suffered as a child. He told me that one of the reasons I had wanted to look like a man was because looking like a girl was what had gotten me hurt in the first place. Immediately, I was set free in my mind. The women in the church showed me lots of love, and God used many of them to encourage and pray for me. I found people I could talk to whenever I was struggling with issues like low self-esteem, rejection, fear, and anger. Having the love, acceptance, and accountability of people made the process a lot easier.

Accountability—the word means responsibility...

After I went through my deliverance, I needed to be accountable to other Christians. Pride will tell us that we don't need others, but God intended for His children to walk together, to be accountable to one another, and to carry one another's burdens. I'm so glad the Lord gave me a balance of men and women who loved Jesus and wanted to help me continue in my healing process. Being accountable to others brought a real transformation in my life. I learned to yield to truth because it was spoken to me in love. They helped me to establish spiritual boundaries in my life and to mature in the Lord, acting as mentors to me. Although their "issues" were different from mine, I believed that the same God who had brought healing into their lives could bring it into mine. I wanted to keep my deliverance, so even in difficult times, I learned to depend upon my heavenly Father's unfailing love and to listen to my brothers and sisters in Christ. As I did this, my true identity became clearer.

What other things were important to me? Prayer and God's words were (and still are) so important in my Christian walk. I have found strength and gained confidence to live, move, and have my being in Him as I commune with God in prayer and spend time reading His Word. They enable me to believe in myself even when other people criticize me. God has used prayer and His Word to change my attitude toward people.

Praying for others also became a very important part of my life. Every Wednesday morning, I would meet with other women at the church for prayer. They always included me, and I was grateful to be part of the group. As I learned how to make "war in the spirit," I realized how many people had needs just like mine and how important it was to pray for others. Some of the women asked me to pray for relatives or friends who were struggling with homosexuality. For a while, no one would openly talk about it because it was a very sensitive subject. But As God continued to strengthen me and give me courage, I began to talk about my experiences, and more people began to ask me to pray. The need was greater than I could have ever imagined. Prayer strengthened my hope for my own life and for others who were trapped in the lifestyle that once held me.

I found myself following the example of Jesus. The Bible says that "Jesus often withdrew Himself and prayed." I began to ask God to give His people a new heart because that's what prayer had done for me in addition to bringing greater measures of peace into my life. Prayer caused me to start trusting God and walk by faith because until I accepted Jesus as my Lord and Savior, I had never seen anyone delivered from homosexuality. When I read about how Father God raised Jesus from the dead, I knew there was hope for me to stay free.

I also began to understand spiritual things, and I started to realize why some people fear homosexuals. One reason is that they are insecure. Another is that some are secretly struggling with homosexuality in their own lives or have family members who are active in the lifestyle. I continued to receive counseling. During one session, I really felt like God wanted me to deal with the anger I held toward men. I didn't realize how much pain I was in until after I received healing in this area. An elder and his wife met with me. I told them what I had been feeling, and they prayed for me. Then came a time of testing. I found myself still resenting men and cried at times because I feared I would never overcome this. But the Lord did a gradual work in my heart. I kept praying, I tried putting my faith into action, and I trusted God. My breakthrough finally came. God gave me the courage and willpower to have victory over my struggle. It took a long time before I stopped getting very angry with men about simple things. In 1 John 1:9, the Word says, "If we (freely) admit that we have sinned and confess our sins, He is faithful and just (true to His own nature and promises) and will forgive our sins and cleanse us continually from all unrighteousness (our wrong-doing, everything not in conformity with His will and purpose)." Whenever I struggled with rage, I would ask someone to pray and believe God with me. It was an act of humility and surrender to Christ, and it really helped me. The more liberty I experienced, the deeper my love for God became, and I began to develop healthy relationships with my brothers in Christ.

2 Corinthians 5:17

Therefore, if anyone is in Christ (that is, grafted in, joined to Him by faith in Him as Savior), he is a new creature (reborn and renewed by the Holy Spirit); the old things (the spiritual moral and spiritual condition) have passed away. Behold, new things have come (because spiritual awakening brings a new life).

Liberation

My attitude started changing, even toward the people who had once offended me. Jesus was teaching me how to forgive others. I wasn't angry at the world anymore, and I realized that God loved me so much that He was offering a better life to me and to my children. Harsh words against me no longer mattered, and I realized that everyone needs God whether they are homosexual or not. God wasn't looking at who I was but who I was to become. As I began to walk in freedom, I experienced joy and peace like never before. The shame was fading away, and I was learning to identify with my womanhood.

I threw away the trophies I'd won as a male impersonator. The more I identified with this new woman, the more joy I felt in my heart. The fear of being laughed at and looked down upon was leaving me. The Lord was cleansing me from the inside, and it was beginning to show on the outside. In **2 Corinthians 3:17** it says, *"Now the Lord is the Spirit, and where the Spirit of the Lord is, there is liberty (emancipation from bondage, true freedom)."* For the first time, I was beginning to fully embrace my femininity and appreciate the woman in me! One time at church, Pastor Kevin spoke a prophetic word over me, telling me I was called to be an evangelist. At the time, I didn't even know what the word "evangelist" meant and had to look it up when I got home. (It is someone who shares the good news of Jesus with others and helps them to meet Him personally!) I found it hard to believe that the Lord had called a person like me to be in ministry. All my life, people had put me down and talked down to me. Slowly but surely, though, I began to feel confident that God (who can do ANYTHING) could use me.

The Lord allowed me to stay away from people or things that could cause me to stumble. I never wanted to lose my passion to serve Him. When I couldn't make it to Wednesday morning prayer, I made it up by going early in the morning to pray with others at 6:00 am. I received so much liberty through praying and being accountable to the people God had surrounded me with! At that point, I needed a lot of love, and I began to understand the purpose of ministry and how to fulfill my call.

One day at work, I overheard co-workers discussing a conference they'd attended in New Orleans. Their enthusiasm about the meeting made me curious. I asked them if they had any tapes of the meetings I could borrow. When I got the tapes and took them home, I saw that the women speakers were coming to a nearby city. I couldn't wait to go. One of the speakers was (evangelist), now Bishop Jacqueline McCullough. She and

I had the same calling, and it got me really excited. When I went to hear her speak, the Holy Spirit worked even deeper in me concerning my womanhood. Afterwards, I found a flea market north of the church and got my nails done. I felt so natural with them. After that, I tried lipstick. I loved my new look!

Months later, I decided to try to wear stockings. I must have torn more than a half dozen pairs! I was used to just pulling up my jeans. It was so hard that I got very frustrated and started crying. My daughter saw me struggling, so she came into the room to help me. She said, "You must be gentle and take your time." Eventually, I got it right. The next thing I wanted to try was shoes with heels. I was used to flat shoes, so it was an adjustment for me. The first time I wore them to work, I had to go to on-the-job training. I did well until the class was over and I tried stepping up some stairs and fell. Although people laughed and made fun of me for the rest of the day, I didn't let it stop me. I was determined to be all that God had planned for me.

My femininity was becoming precious to me, and I couldn't help but look at myself in the mirror. One morning, while I was getting ready for work, I began to cry. I looked deeply at myself and saw the woman in me, and I knew I could never be intimate with another woman again. Joy filled my heart. I touched my arms and my face and said, "God, is this really happening to me? Am I dreaming? Because if I am, please don't wake me up!" I began to share my story with my co-workers, and to my surprise, I found out that some of them had family members who were struggling with homosexuality. They had a lot of questions. I didn't know that God was preparing me for a television interview using most of the questions that they asked! My testimony about God's awesome love and delivering power filled my conversations, and soon after this, I had someone prepare a little brochure for me. I gave copies of it to everyone I knew. One of my co-workers sent it to *The 700 Club* (a Christian television ministry), and I received an invitation to share my testimony on the show.

When I arrived in Virginia Beach for the interview, I was somewhat nervous. A very nice gentleman met me at the airport and took me to the studio, where he introduced me to the staff. We had lunch before he took me to my hotel. I had to be in the studio early the next morning for the interview. I prepared myself in prayer, asking God to give me strength to speak His words. I wanted to please Him so much! The next morning, I went to the studio and saw that they actually had a live audience. Some of the questions Terry asked me were the same ones I'd gotten from my co-workers. With the help of the Holy Spirit, the interview went very well. I left shortly afterwards and returned home that evening.

Shortly after my return, I started receiving phone calls and letters from people all over the world! Opportunities began to pour in, and I realized how important it was to stay connected to other believers who would pray for me, give me wise counsel, and hold me accountable. No matter how much we have or how much we accomplish, we still need God's guidance and discernment.

Ephesians 5:8

For once you were darkness, but now you are Light in the Lord; Walk as children of Light (live as those who are native-born to the Light).

Seeing the Extremes

As God continued to light the path He'd set before me, I realized that the church needed more understanding when addressing the issue of homosexuality. I was led to attend a large conference on "Love and Acceptance" in Atlanta, Georgia. I wasn't sure why I needed to be at this conference, except to be a walking example of God's great delivering power to other people who struggle with their sexual identity and desire to be healed and made whole. The conference had already started when I arrived. A handful of people were leading a panel discussion on the issue of homosexuality. One man in the group said, "We cannot literally take the Word of God for what it says." The leader of the group also made it clear that he believed God loved and accepted people right where they were and that he felt there was no need for people to turn away from the homosexual lifestyle. My heart was broken, and a righteous anger began to stir in me. I thought, *This is how people can take the Word of God out of context and use it to justify their behavior.*

Part of what he'd said was true—God does love people with such a great love. But the other part was a lie. Again, we see the need for balance between mercy and truth! This man only wanted to see God's mercy and not His truth. I've known other religious people who want to see God's truth (to judge others) and not His mercy. Both extremes fall short of God's plan. Over time, I came to realize how few churches ever dealt with the issues of homosexuality or deliverance. Often, after I spoke about my own deliverance, Christians would ask me what I was talking about. I would show them **Ephesians 6:12**, which says, *"For our struggle is not against flesh and blood (contending only with physical opponents), but against the rulers, against the powers, against the world forces of this (present) darkness, against the spiritual forces of wickedness in the heavenly (supernatural) places."* Several times after I'd given my testimony, people came up and told me that they had never heard anyone preach about God loving the homosexual, I couldn't believe the hard feelings some church people had against the homosexual community.

One time, someone told me that I shouldn't tell my testimony—that it should be between me and God. I didn't listen to them, though! God's Word says that the followers of Christ overcome Satan by the blood of the Lamb and by the word of their testimony! It's an honor to glorify God. Considering all the great things He has already done for me, this is the least I can do for Him! There have also been times when I gave my testimony and people in the church didn't believe God could deliver a person from homosexuality. They made comments like, "Once a homosexual, always a homosexual." God was slowly opening my eyes to the lack of knowledge and under-standing in the body of Christ (the church) when it pertained to people struggling with their sexual identity.

I went to a support group for people who were ex-homosex-uals one day, and a lady there said that she was looking for answers but she couldn't tell her pastor that she was an ex-les-bian, so she secretly attended the support group. My heart was grieved. I'm so glad that I have a friend in Jesus; otherwise, the smart comments that some preachers make from the pulpit about homosexuals would have sent me running back to the arms of a woman! But once someone is set free, how do they maintain that freedom? The Word says, "Be renewed in the spirit of your mind." When we come to Jesus, accept who He is, and believe He purchased freedom for us, He comes and makes His home inside us. We then have the power to change our thoughts (for much of the battle is in the mind!). When our thoughts change, our actions and our behavior change as well. Being transformed is not a momentary experience; rather, it is an ongoing process.

1 Corinthians 6:9-11a

Do you not know that the unrighteous will not inherit or have any share in the kingdom of God? Do not be deceived: Neither the sexually immortal, nor, idolaters, nor adulterers, nor effemi-nate, (by perversion) nor those who participate in homosexuality nor thieves nor the greedy nor drunkards nor revilers (whose words are used as weapons to abuse, insult, humiliate, intimi-date, or slander), nor swindlers will inherit or have any share in the Kingdom of God. And such were some of you (before you believed).

The passage above is from a letter written by Paul the Apostle to the Christians in the city of Corinth. Paul wrote that some of those Christians used to be adulterers, male prosti-tutes, idolaters, homosexuals, thieves, drunkards, etc., but that something had happened, and they had changed! Once they accepted Jesus, they had the power of the Holy Spirit within them to help them stay free. He gave them the power to defeat old strongholds of thought and habit.

2 Corinthians 10:3-5

For though we walk in the flesh (as mortal men), we are not car-rying on our (spiritual) warfare according to the flesh and using the weapons of man. The weapons of our warfare are not physical (weapons of flesh and blood). Our weapons are divinely powerful for the destruction of fortresses. We are destroying sophisticated arguments and every exalted and proud thing that sets itself up against the (true) knowledge of God and we are taking every thought and purpose captive to the obedience of Christ.

I am determined to hold on to my faith—or better said, to let Jesus hold on to me. And I ask Him to help me pray for the whole church. Thank God there have been times when I've preached and people have actually come up and led everyone into repentance over how they have treated homosexuals. It is essential for the church to wake up, as the issue of homosexuality is becoming a large one.

Isaiah 61:1

The Spirit of the Lord God is upon me, Because the Lord has anointed and commissioned me to bring good news to the humble and afflicted. He has sent me to bind up (the wounds of) the brokenhearted, To proclaim release (from confinement and condemnation) to the (physical and spiritual) captives and freedom to prisoners.

It's time for the church to stand up and take its rightful position. God is love, and He demonstrated that love when He sent His one and only begotten Son to suffer, bleed, and die on the cross for the world. In God's eyes, homosexuality is no different from any other sin, and God loves the sinner. I am a true witness of His unconditional love!

Helping Others Start Their Journey at a Women's

Correctional Institution

We began processing into the prison and headed to the chapel. A young lady approached us and said, "I know that God sent you because I felt the presence of God on my way here." About 300 women came to the meeting, and I told them how I had lived a lesbian lifestyle as a male impersonator for twenty years before I was set free by the power of God. As I continued sharing about my life, I noticed a young lady in the room standing to my right with her arms folded. I had to look twice because she looked like a man. Many were healed and set free by the power of God. And when the Lord's power is present, evil spirits who are oppressing and using people are often revealed.

I began to walk among the women and pray. The young lady who'd been standing with her arms folded fell on the floor and began to slither on her back like a serpent. We gathered around her to pray while the Lord set her free from this demonic influence. Then I continued on and ministered to others who were also being set free from evil spirits. At the end of the service, I looked for the young lady because I wanted to talk to her. When I did see her, I didn't recognize her because her countenance had changed! I saw peace on her face and a glow that hadn't been there before. I knew it was the glory of God.

Two weeks later, I received a call from the minister who had invited me to speak. She told me that many women in the institution had heard about my testimony and were curious, so they began showing up at the Bible study at the facility. At the study, the young lady who had been so wonderfully delivered shared her testimony, and many others were set free as well.

A Home for Boys

A gain, I was invited to share my story of how the power of God had changed my life. Before I began to share my experience, the Lord had me pray out loud. I felt in my heart that many of the boys had issues and were looking for answers. I was told that a week before I got to the facility, a young man had attempted to sexually assault two boys. I wanted to make sure that I spoke only the words that God would have me speak. I looked out as I spoke and knew He was already healing hearts. As I looked out over the crowd, I could see signs of relief on many faces. When I asked if anyone wanted prayer, I felt drawn to one young man who was about six feet tall. Several of us began to pray for him, and he fell, letting out a scream I will never forget. The Lord showed me he had an effeminate spirit. I later found out that he was the young man involved with the two boys. He began to pour out his heart, thanking God and us for helping him.

Naples High Football Stadium, Naples, FL, National Day of Prayer

I'd been invited to stand and pray for personal renewal and moral awakening. An estimated 1,500 people turned out for the event, including the mayor and other community leaders. Tommie Tennie was the keynote speaker. When my turn came to pray for our country, I briefly shared the hope of God and how He had delivered me from homosexuality. When the event was winding down, many parents who had children struggling with their sexual identity came up and embraced me, weeping and praising God. They had lots of questions and continued to say how grateful they were to God for using me to bring hope to them. I began to weep. I suddenly realized how desperate people were for the truth. On my way back to the car, a group of teenagers stopped and asked if they could pray for me. I humbly said, "Yes." Their prayers were so precious and so powerful as they asked God to please keep me strong.

Key West, FL.

A local women's fellowship had invited me to be their speaker. I really felt that God was going to do something special, but He didn't reveal exactly what it was until I got there. After I checked into my room, I began to worship the Lord and seek His face for strength to do what He had purposed in me. When the time came for me to speak, I shared about hope and healing from homosexuality. As I began praying for people, God began speaking directly to people through me. I passed by one woman, but before I could speak to the next person, I turned to the woman and said, "The Lord told me to tell you that the curse is broken." She began screaming and running. Later, I passed by as she stood against the wall, weeping. She said, "Please pray for me. I am a married woman, and I've struggled with lesbianism." She told me that she didn't want to be gay and that she, too, was looking for the truth. God heard her prayer and used me to tell her she was free.

Genesis 18:14

"Is anything too difficult or too wonderful for the Lord?"

In Conclusion

D o I believe that all homosexuals and people suffering from problems with their sexual identity are that way for the same reasons? No. Do I think they suffer because of mental illness, the result of molestation or abuse, a physical problem, demonic forces, rebellion, or curses? In my own life and in listening to the stories of others, I've found that there is no one size that fits all. Most often, people have a combination of circumstances and attitudes which have worked together to create the end result. But I have faith that God can set any person free of any problem, regardless of the cause.

> **Matthew 4:23-24** says, *"And He went throughout all Galilee, teaching in their synagogues and preaching the good news (gospel) of the kingdom, and healing every kind of disease and every kind of sickness among the people (demonstrating and revealing that He was indeed the promised Messiah). So the news about Him spread throughout all Syria; and they brought to Him all who were sick, those*

suffering with various diseases and pains, those under the power of demons and epileptics, paralytics; and He healed them." It didn't matter what was wrong in someone's life—whether they were sick with a disease, tormented, were lunatics, or had demons, He healed them all! Nothing is too big or too small for Jesus. He set me free, and I know He can do it for others. If I do nothing more than bring someone into His presence, I've brought them to the very best place. Because if anyone comes to know the Truth (Jesus), the Truth shall set them free.

You may be asking, where do I start? Throughout time, when people wanted to communicate with God, they built an altar, a place to meet with Him. In this time, people may attend a church and hear an invitation to "come to the altar" in the front of the church to pray. But God longs to make His tabernacle in your heart, and the altar (where you decide what to do or not do, who to serve or not serve) is already in your heart. You can invite Jesus, even now, to visit you at the altar in your heart, and you can be forever ALTERED—changed. You can begin your journey this very moment from right where you are. Pray with your heart:

Dear Heavenly Father,

> I believe Your Son, Jesus, died for my sins, and that He was buried and rose again as it is written in the Bible. I am sorry for the things I have done that hurt You. Forgive me for all my sins. Jesus, come into my heart, take charge of my life, and make me the way You want me to be. With Your ever-present help, I renounce all my sinful practices of the past. Please cleanse my heart with Your precious blood and write my name in Your Book of Life! I confess You now as my Lord and Savior. Fill me with Your precious Holy Spirit. Thank you, Jesus! In Jesus's name, Amen.

I am the founder and President of Out of The Fire, Inc. We are a non-profit organization/ministry that bring hope and healing to people from all walks of life. I attended seminary under the leadership of Apostle Kevin McAnulty. I am ordained, licensed and also recognized as an Evangelist. We have an on-line Bible study/Facebook that starts at 04:00 am Sunday- Friday. I minister the Word through prayers, testimonials, the spoken word of God, scriptures for today and words of encouragement. I have also traveled the states preaching and teaching the Word of God. I have appeared on The 700 Club, an Affiliate for Trinity Broadcasting Network, Atlanta

57 and several other local Christian Television and Radio stations. I was also featured in Charisma magazine.

My Prayer For Those Who Struggle:

Dear Father God,

Thank you for Your unfailing love toward Your people. I was once powerless over my sin, but because of Your grace, mercy, and truth, I can now hold my head up, not in pride but in confidence of my true identity. Lord, I pray a special prayer for those who are caught in the homosexual lifestyle. I pray for their eyes to be opened and their hearts to understand that there is no condemnation at the cross. You allowed Your Son to suffer and die so that we could walk in wholeness as men and women of God. Help them to see and to receive Your truth...and Your mercy. In Jesus's name, Amen.

CPSIA information can be obtained
at www.ICGtesting.com
Printed in the USA
BVHW052229110523
664021BV00010B/138

9 781662 876936